T0090510

I Am a Child of Abraham

of Abraham

A Thirty-One-Day Devotional and Prayer to Help Build and Strengthen Your Faith

Dr. Valerie Dye

WestBow
PRESS®
A DIVISION OF THOMAS NELSON
& ZONDERVAN

This book is a work of non-fiction. Unless otherwise noted, the author
and the publisher make no explicit guarantees as to the accuracy of
the information contained in this book and in some cases, names
of people and places have been altered to protect their privacy.

WestBow Press books may be ordered through booksellers or by contacting:

WestBow Press
A Division of Thomas Nelson & Zondervan
1663 Liberty Drive
Bloomington, IN 47403
www.westbowpress.com
844-714-3454

Because of the dynamic nature of the Internet, any web addresses or
links contained in this book may have changed since publication and
may no longer be valid. The views expressed in this work are solely those
of the author and do not necessarily reflect the views of the publisher,
and the publisher hereby disclaims any responsibility for them.

Scripture taken from the Holy Bible, New International Version®.
NIV®. Copyright © 1973, 1978, 1984 by International Bible
Society. Used by permission of Zondervan. All rights reserved.

Scripture taken from King James version of the Bible.

Any people depicted in stock imagery provided by Getty Images are models,
and such images are being used for illustrative purposes only.
Certain stock imagery © Getty Images.

ISBN: 979-8-3850-0104-0 (sc)
ISBN: 979-8-3850-0105-7 (e)

Library of Congress Control Number: 2023911816

Print information available on the last page.

WestBow Press rev. date: 06/23/2023

Contents

Introduction

The devotionals in this book contain Bible stories and scriptures that will help build and strengthen your faith in the Lord. There is nothing that God cannot do, but we are often limited by our lack of faith. As you read these devotionals each day, you will be reminded that we serve an all-powerful God who can do above and beyond what we can ask and imagine. It simply requires our faith.

Day 1

ABRAHAM'S JOURNEY OF FAITH

Go from your country, your people and your father's household to the land I will show you.

—Genesis 12:1–4 (NIV)

When God lays it upon our hearts to do something, do we wait until we have clearer instructions before responding? Are you afraid to move because you do not see the end result of the process?

In Genesis 12:1–4, God clearly wanted to bless Abraham. He told Abraham to leave his comfortable dwelling and go to a land he would show him. What is fascinating about that scripture is that God did not tell Abraham where he was going. We know that he ended up in the Land of Canaan, but God told Abraham to go to a land that "I will show you." Abraham was required to just go. The Bible does not tell us that Abraham asked God which direction he should go. He didn't ask for a map; he didn't ask for a blueprint or an address. All Abraham needed was an assurance that God told him to go and that God will be with him and bless him.

We live in a culture where one is required to have all the details before moving forward. We need to know the feasibility of a project before beginning. However, with

God, all we need is the assurance that he is with us, that he has directed us, and that he will see us through. We do not need the blueprint. Moving in faith requires complete trust in God that once he directs us, he will take us to the promise.

Abraham obeyed the voice of God without knowing the details of where he was going. In response to his faith, God blessed him abundantly.

My Prayer

Father, thank you for the example of your servant Abraham. Give me the strength to hold on to your word and move in faith, believing that you are able to do in my life what you promised to do. I believe you are able to bless me abundantly as I move in faith and receive my blessings in Jesus's name.

Day 2

IF I PERISH, I PERISH

I will go to the king even though it is
against the law and if I perish I perish.
—Esther 4:16 (NIV)

Esther replaced Queen Vashti as the wife of King Ahasuerus.
King Ahasuerus did not know that Esther was a Jew, but he
chose her out of many other women who had vied for the
opportunity to become queen.

The time came when the king passed a decree to destroy
all the Jews in the land because of the evil plot of Haman,
the king's chief officer. All of the Jews, including Esther's
uncle Mordecai, went into mourning because of this decree.
Someone needed to plead with the king on behalf of the
Jews. Who better than Queen Esther to do so? After all,
she was the wife of the king, and she was a Jew. Surely, she
should be the one to plead the cause of the Jews and save
them from destruction.

There was only one problem with that picture. No one
could go before the king unless he summoned them. If
anyone went before the king without being summoned, that
person would be killed unless he lifted his golden scepter.
Esther was faced with a dilemma. She knew she had to try
and save her people, but she also did not wish to die.

The next step that Esther needed to take required
boldness, courage, and faith. She called a fast and instructed

all the Jews to fast with her for three days. At the end of three days, she was fully emboldened and full of faith.

She decided that she would go before the king and said to her uncle, "I will go to the king which is against the law and if I perish I perish." What a bold move! As a result of Esther's boldness and courage, the Jews were saved from destruction.

Notice that Esther did not rush into the king's presence and say, "If I perish, I perish." She sought the Lord in fasting and praying and received strength and courage from him. There may be times in our lives when we may be required to make tough choices like the one Esther had to make. When this happens, we should ask God to strengthen and be with us. Once we know that God is with us, we will be able to face any difficult situation head-on.

My Prayer

Father, I come before you today and ask for boldness and courage to do whatever I need in every situation. Help me to remember that even when a situation seems hopeless and likely to lead to destruction, you are able to turn it around. Help me to face difficult circumstances not in my own strength but from the strength and courage drawn from you.

Day 3

DO NOT CRY OUT TO ME

> Why do you cry out to me? Tell the children
> of Israel to go forward.
> —Exodus 14:15 (ESV)

Can you imagine what it must have been like for the children of Israel when they escaped from Egypt and came to the Red Sea? They were stuck between the Egyptian army which was quickly overtaking them and the Red Sea which was before them. There was absolutely no place to go unless they went into the sea and drowned. But God had brought them out of Egypt with his mighty hand. He was not about to let them down now. Yet in their carnal and finite minds, they could not envisage how God would deliver them at this moment when the sea was before them. This was indeed the end—or at least in their minds.

Their salvation required them to move forward. In Exodus 14:15–16, the Lord said to Moses,

> Why are you crying out to me? Tell the
> Israelites to go forward. Raise your staff and
> stretch out your hand over the sea to divide
> it that the people of Israel may go through
> the sea on dry ground. (ESV)

The Lord is not saying that we should never cry out to him. He says that we need to move forward in faith based on his word and promise to us. He had already given the children of Israel the victory. They needed to move forward in faith. We can liken the Red Sea to any impossible situation in our lives. God is the God of the impossible, and if we believe and move in faith, he can turn the seas in our lives into dry land.

My Prayer

Father, I come before you in the name of Jesus Christ. I thank you that you are the God of the impossible. No matter how difficult or impossible a situation seems, you are able to deliver me. I put my complete faith and trust in you and thank you for the breakthrough in my life.

Day 4

HE IS ENOUGH

> I am the bread of life; whoever comes to me
> shall not hunger, and whoever believes in
> me shall never thirst.
>
> —John 6:35 (ESV)

Do you sometimes feel that you are alone? Do you often feel destitute and hopeless and that there is no one to turn to? Jesus is enough!

In John 6:35 (ESV), Jesus said,

> I am the bread of Life. Whoever comes to
> me shall never hunger; and he that believes
> in me shall never thirst.

This refers to both spiritual hunger and thirst and physical hunger and thirst. Of course naturally, we will be hungry and thirsty, but this verse tells us that Jesus will provide all our physical and spiritual needs.

The Bible also tells us that we will lack nothing. Psalm 23 (NIV) says,

> The Lord is my shepherd, I lack nothing.

Psalm 34:10 (ESV) says,

> The young lions suffer want and hunger;
> but those who seek the LORD lack no good
> thing.

You see, once we put our faith and trust in Jesus and live for him, he becomes our provider, our healer, our deliverer, our very present help in times of need (Psalm 45), our friend who sticks closer than a brother, our burden bearer and joy giver, our comforter, and our shield.

He is, indeed, enough!

My Prayer

Father, I confess that often I do feel alone and hopeless, but I thank you for your word that reminds me that you are enough. Once I put my faith and trust in you, I will lack nothing. Today, I look to you as my provider, comforter, hope, and strength. I thank you that you never fail.

Day 5

DO YOU BELIEVE?

> If you can believe, all things are possible to
> him who believes.
> > —Mark 9:23 (NKJV)

Jesus performed many miracles while he walked on Earth. In Matthew 9:27, two blind men approached Jesus and asked him to have mercy on them. Jesus responded with a question,

Do you believe that I can do this?

When they responded that they believed, Jesus touched and healed them.

In Mark 9:11 (NKJV), Jesus told the father of the boy who had a mute spirit,

> If you can believe, all things are possible to
> him who believes.

The father not only said that he believed, but he asked Jesus to help his unbelief. He was asking for an increase in his faith.

The foundation of the Christian life is based on belief in the Lord Jesus Christ. Hebrews 11: 7 (NKJV) says,

> He who comes to God must believe that
> he is and that he is a rewarder of those who
> diligently seek him.

Our beliefs should not depend on what we see. After Jesus was raised from the dead, some disciples doubted the account of those who claimed they had seen him. Jesus then appeared to the eleven disciples and rebuked them because they did not believe those who had seen him after he had risen. Mark 16:14 says that "he rebuked their unbelief and hardness of heart."

Even after we come to him, we must continue to believe that he is able to heal, deliver, provide, and do all that we ask. Without this, it is impossible to please him; and without belief, we ask in vain. This is why all of Jesus's miracles are premised on the faith of those who received healing.

The woman with the issue of blood had so much faith that she felt that a mere touch of his garment could heal her. Touched by her faith, Jesus said, "Your faith has made you well."

It is our lack of faith that limits us. Where we lack belief, we should do as the father of the deaf boy did and say, "Lord, help my unbelief." Even the disciples asked Jesus in Luke 17:5 to increase their faith.

God can do anything we ask, but it is up to us to believe so that we can receive.

My Prayer

Father, I come to you today with praise and thanksgiving. I believe that you are able to heal and deliver. I ask that where I lack the belief that you help my unbelief. I now receive your healing and deliverance, and I rejoice at the work of your hands in Jesus's name.

Day 6

STEP OUT OF THE BOAT

> Lord, if it is You, command me to come to
> You on the water.
> —Matthew 14:28 (ESV)

Peter is often described as "impetuous and hasty," yet what
a lesson of faith we can learn from him. When he saw Jesus
walking on water, he cried out to him,

> Lord, if it is You, command me to come to
> You on the water. (Matthew 15:28 ESV)

All Peter needed to know was that it was his Lord who
was walking on the water. It was enough for him to step out
of the boat. Notice that he first ensured that it was Jesus who
was on the water. He made sure that when he stepped out
of that boat, Jesus would be with him. Not only that, but
he would be in the will of Jesus, he would be doing what he
was commanded to do. Jesus said to Peter, "Yes, come"; and
without hesitating, Peter stepped out of the boat.

Would you be so bold as to step into a dangerous
situation if you are assured that God is with you?

Are you hesitant to make a bold and unconventional
decision? Something that is outside of the norm? Do not
let fear inhibit you. Like Peter, make sure that you will act
within God's will. Make sure that it is something that God

will have you do. Seek his face to know his will and purpose for your life. Once you are assured that God will be with you, put aside all doubt and fear, step out in faith, and keep your eyes on Jesus. God will honor your faith and keep you afloat even in the roughest storm.

My Prayer

Dear Lord, I come to you today in the name of Jesus Christ. I lay aside every fear or doubt that has plagued my mind; and I stand upon your promise, knowing that whatever you have called me to do, you will see me through. I take my eyes off the circumstances around me, and I focus only on your word. I thank you that as I hold on to your word and your promise, I can do whatever you have called me to do. I ask for boldness and courage as I step into whatever you have called me to do.

Day 7

THEY WERE CLEANSED

> When he saw them, he said, "Go, show
> yourselves to the priests. And as they went,
> they were cleansed."
> —Luke 17:11–19 (NIV)

On his way to Jerusalem, Jesus was heading into a village where he met ten men who had leprosy. They stood at a distance as was required at that time for people afflicted with leprosy. They cried out to Jesus to have pity on them. They needed healing.

It would be normal to expect Jesus to lay hands on the lepers and heal them, just as he had done with others. Perhaps Jesus wanted to test their faith. Instead of laying hands on them, he told them to show themselves to the priest. The men walked off, and as they went, they were healed.

What if they had turned away, disappointed that Jesus did not lay hands on them or command the leprosy to leave? They would not have been healed. Their healing came as they went off in obedience to God's words. Our answers from God will not always come in natural ways. All that may be required is a simple act of obedience done in faith.

A similar story takes place with Naaman in 2 Kings 5:1–17. Naaman was stricken with leprosy. When Elijah told him to wash seven times in the Jordan River, he was angry.

He thought that Elisha would come out and stand in front of him and call on the name of the Lord. Naaman almost missed his healing as he was about to turn away in anger and resentment. His servants stepped in and encouraged him to obey Elisha. Naaman decided to do as Elisha had told him, and in doing so, he obtained his healing.

God may often ask us to do unconventional things that may seem strange to others. If we trust him, we will do as he asks us to do because he is indeed faithful to bring to pass whatever we are seeking him for.

My Prayer

Father, I thank you that you work in many different ways. I ask that you help me to act in obedience even when it requires doing something unusual. Help me not to miss what you want to do in my life because I expect things to be done a certain way. I declare today that I will draw closer to you so that I will be more in tune with your ways and direction for my life. I thank you today for your faithfulness.

Day 8

THE SCARLET CORD

For the Lord you God is God in heaven
above and on the earth below.
—Joshua 2:11(NIV)

Joshua sent his men to spy on Jericho in preparation for
the attack. The men ended up in the home of the prostitute
Rahab. The Bible does not tell us when the men went to
that home. Nonetheless, Rahab had heard of how the God
of the Israelites had done exploits for them. In fact, everyone
in Jericho had heard of those exploits, and they trembled
in fear.

The men in Rahab's house were the enemies of the
people of Jericho, and here they were at the mercy of Rahab.
She could do anything to them at this point, even kill them
or turn them over to the king of Jericho. She could have
also set a trap for the rest of the army who would invade the
land. But Rahab already knew that the God of Israel was the
true and living God. She had enough faith and trust in his
strength to deliver that she knew that even if she had turned
the men over, their God would save them.

By faith, she chose to forsake her country and people
because she believed in the power of the God of Israel to
save her.

Rahab was assured that once she hung a scarlet cord on
the window of her home, she would be saved. Once the men

saw that cord, they would not destroy her home. It required great faith for Rahab to put her trust in a simple scarlet cord. Nonetheless, her faith paid off, and she and her household were saved.

That scarlet cord is symbolic of the blood of Jesus. All we need is to have faith in the power of the shed blood of Jesus, and we will be saved. Because of her faith, Rahab and her family were saved when she placed a scarlet cord on the window of their home. Because of our faith, God will keep and protect us.

My Prayer

Father, I thank you for the shed blood of Jesus. Because of that shed blood, I am victorious over the plans of the enemy. I place my complete rust on the finished work on the cross and receive victory in every situation that affects my life. I believe that I am an overcomer by the blood of Jesus, and I thank you for the victory in the precious name of Jesus.

GOD GIVES, BUT WE MUST POSSESS

See, I have given Jericho into your hand,
with its king and mighty men of valor.
—Joshua 6:1–27 (ESV)

The children of Israel were about to cross the River Jordan. God gave them the assurance that he had given into their hands the city of Jericho and its inhabitants. They already had the promise, but it was not yet manifested to them. They had to do something in order to possess what God had given them in the spirit.

They were required to go around the walls of Jericho once for six days, and on the seventh day, they were required to go around seven times. They not only had to march, but they had to take their musical instruments and the ark, and then they had to shout. It was only after all this that the walls came down.

Why didn't God bring the walls down immediately and allow them to invade the land? He had already told them he had given it to them, hadn't he? Well, God had, indeed, given them the land of Jericho in the spirit; but for this to be manifested physically, they had to exercise faith in order to possess what God had already given to them.

Imagine being left an inheritance in your father's will.

Your father dies, and you read the will and discover you have been left one million dollars. That one million dollars is yours, but you don't have it in your bank account. You may start rejoicing and celebrating because you have it, but unless you take steps to possess it, you still remain in financial lack. To obtain that one million dollars, you must first believe it is there and then take the necessary steps to possess it.

In the same way, God gives us a blessing, but we have to possess that blessing to enjoy it. To possess what is already ours, we need to take it in faith, which requires action.

My Prayer

Father, I thank you for the many blessings you have provided for me. Thank you for showing me in your word that I need to take steps to possess what you have already provided. I know you have already provided for my financial well-being, health, prosperity, and more. I intend to move in faith to possess all that you have provided so that I can enjoy everything that you have given me. I thank you today for your love and your provision. In Jesus's name, amen.

Day 10

MORE THAN WE CAN IMAGINE

Now you shall see whether what I say will
happen to you or not.
—Numbers 11:23 (NJKV)

How many times do we believe God for a miracle, yet in our
finite minds, we try to figure out natural ways to how God
will perform that miracle?

Numbers 11 tells us that this is exactly what Moses did.
The children of Israel complained about food and compared
their lives in the wilderness to their time in Egypt when
they had so much good food. The Lord, in his anger, sent
fire among them. He then told Moses that he would send
food to the people not for one day or two days but for an
entire month so that they would eat until it came out of their
nostrils. The Lord was, indeed, angry.

Moses tried to imagine how God would provide so
much food for many people. His response was in itself one of
doubt. He said to the Lord, "Here I am among six hundred
thousand men on foot, and you say you will give them
meat to eat for a whole month! Would they have enough
if flocks and herds were slaughtered for them? Would they
have enough if all the fish in the sea were caught for them?"

In his finite mind, Moses could not imagine how God would feed so many people for an entire month.

The Lord responded, "Is the Lord's hand waxed short? You will now see whether or not what I say will come true for you."

In other words, God was saying, "You do not need to figure out how I will do what I said I would do."

In verse 31, we see that God caused a great wind to blow quail from the sea, and there was so much quail that the people gathered quail all day and all night.

Sometimes we are like Moses. God gives us a promise, or we believe him for a miracle, and we try to figure out how this will happen. The promise seems so impossible that we begin to question how this can happen. Sometimes we even try to help God. Our attitude should be "God said it, and he will do it." We do not need to know how he will do it. He is God.

My Prayer

Thank you, Father, for your awesome power. You are an infinite God, and our finite minds cannot conceive how you will work. I ask forgiveness for the times I have placed limits on you because of the limits of my mind. Help me to remember that you are limitless and can do all things. It is not up to me to figure out how you will do it. I believe that you will do what you said you will, and I thank you for doing it.

Day 11

FAITH AND ACTION

As the Body without the Spirit is dead, so
faith without deeds is dead.
                                    —James 2:26 (NIV)

It is common to hear people say that they trust God for
things, whether it be their healing, finances, or marriage.
Yet many times this trust is not accompanied by action to
change their situation. Many Christians think that all they
need to do is trust God, believe him, and do nothing else.
This is sometimes true when there is nothing else one can
do. Nonetheless, faith and action go hand in hand. We must
exercise our faith through our actions. James 2 outlines this
clearly in verses 21–22 (NIV):

> Was not our father Abraham considered
> righteous for what he did when he offered
> his son Isaac on the altar? You see that his
> faith and his actions were working together,
> and his faith was made complete by what
> he did.

James reminds us that a person is justified by what he
does and not by faith alone. If we say we have faith in God
to come through for us but do not put this faith into action,
our faith is incomplete. We may believe that God will heal

our finances. This may require starting a business. We may believe in God for healing. This may require changing our lifestyle. We may see our brother and sister in need. To meet this need, we might have to do more than pray for them. We feed them if they are in need of food or clothe them if they are in need of clothes. Faith must be accompanied by action.

Rahab knew that the God of the Israelites was all-powerful and that he was able to save her and her household. In faith, she provided accommodation to Joshua's men, hid them from the king of Jericho, and protected them. Her faith was accompanied by action, and she was counted as righteous. Furthermore, it was Rehab's faith combined with her actions that produced results.

As we continue to have faith and trust in the Lord, let us remember to combine our faith with action so that we can enjoy the blessings that God has stored up for us.

My Prayer

Dear Lord, I come before you in the precious name of Jesus, and I thank you for your word. I thank you that your promises are true. I thank you for your faithfulness. Where I have failed to act in accordance with your word, I ask your forgiveness. I ask for strength to apply action to faith and take steps to see your promises bear fruit in my life. From here onward, I will put my faith into action, and I thank you for what you are about to do in my life as a result.

Day 12

THE LOVE CONNECTION

And now these three remain: faith, hope
and love. But the greatest of these is love.
—1 Corinthians 13:13 (NIV)

In writing to the Galatians, Paul mentioned that there was
no value in adopting the Jewish practice of circumcision. He
wrote in Galatians 5:6 (NIV) that

> for in Christ Jesus neither circumcision nor
> uncircumcision has any value. The only
> thing that counts is faith expressing itself
> through love.

This scripture tells us that there is a connection between
faith and love. Paul tells us that we need love in order to
express our faith in God. This is no surprise because the
Bible tells us that God is love. The epitome of his character
is love, so if we are to follow him and be in Him, we must
also love. 1 John 4:8 (NIV) says, "Whoever does not love,
does not know God, because God is love."

Here is the connection: we come to God through faith,
wherein we believe that he exists. As it says in Hebrews 11:6
(NIV),

> And without faith it is impossible to please
> God, because anyone who comes to him
> must believe that he exists and that he
> rewards those who earnestly seek him.

However, we cannot separate faith from love because it is impossible to know God through faith if we do not have love.

We must not only love God but also love one another. In 1 John 4:7,11, the Bible encourages us to love one another. Jesus himself also commanded his disciples to love one another. He said in John 13:34–35 (NIV):

> Love one another. As I have loved you, so
> you must love one another. By this, everyone
> will know that you are my disciples, if you
> love one another.

Prophecies will cease, tongues will be stilled, and knowledge will pass away; but only faith, hope, and love will remain. Paul tells us that of those three, love is the greatest.

As we draw near to God in faith, let us remember that love is the connecting thread that gives us access to him.

My Prayer

Dear Father, thank you for loving me so much that you sent your Son to die on the cross for me. I ask now that you help me to love you more and others. Your word says that you are love, and unless we love, we cannot know you. My desire is to know you more, so I ask that you touch my heart so that I will learn to love more. In Jesus's name, amen.

Day 13

WE WILL HAVE
WHAT WE SAY

> Truly I tell you, if anyone says to this mountain, "Go, throw yourself into the sea," and does not doubt in their heart but believes that what they say will happen, it will be done for them.
>
> —Mark 11:23 (NIV)

Our words can shape our circumstances. Negative words can lead to negative outcomes. Most of us know about the power of words. To what extent do we act on that knowledge? Jesus assures us of the authority we have to speak to situations and see them change. In Mark 11:23 (NIV), Jesus illustrates how we can speak to situations in our lives.

When Jesus was hungry, he and his disciples approached a fig tree and discovered it had no fruit. Jesus cursed the fig tree and declared that no one would eat from it again. The following day, the disciples were startled to discover that the fig tree had died. Jesus used this as an illustration to his disciples and to us today about the power of our words. He said to them,

Truly I tell you, if anyone says to this mountain, "Go throw yourself into the sea," and does not doubt in their heart but believes that what they say will happen, it will be done for them.

The word *mountain* can represent any situation in our lives that seems formidable. It may be sickness, financial issues, or even broken relationships. The power to speak to situations is not only to destroy but also to build up. We can have what we say if we truly believe. We can speak to our circumstances. We can command sickness and disease to leave our bodies. We can truly have what we say once we believe in our hearts that we can have it.

My Prayer

Father, you have shown in your word that we can speak to our situations. You have given us the authority to rebuke sickness, poverty, and every negative situation in our lives. Today, I stand upon the authority given to me by Jesus Christ, and I command every situation (call them by name) to disappear in the name of Jesus.

Day 14

THIS MOUNTAIN
SHALL BE MOVED

Who are you, O great mountain? Before
Zerubbabel you shall become a plain.
                    —Zechariah 4:7 (ESV)

Zerubbabel was the leader of the exiled Jews who returned
to Jerusalem. They began constructing the temple, but
this project was soon halted because of opposition from
neighboring peoples. Hope was lost, and the people became
discouraged. The Lord spoke to Zerubbabel, reminding him
that the temple would be built not by might or by power but
by his spirit. Zechariah 4:7 uses the analogy of a mountain
becoming plain to illustrate how God will destroy every
opposition and obstacle. And he will do so by his spirit, not
through our abilities.

Zerubbabel must have become so discouraged that he
felt that even if the temple were to be completed, he might
not be the one to complete it. God assured him that he,
Zerubbabel, had laid the foundation of this temple; his
hands shall also finish it.

This is a reminder that when all hope seems lost, God
can still use us. First, the reminder is that it is not our efforts
that will accomplish anything but it is by the power of the
Holy Spirit. Second, no matter how great the obstacle is,

God can break it down. He can turn our mountains into plains. All we need to do is to trust him.

We may be discouraged by the slow pace with which things are happening. We may give up on projects that seem to have been stalled. God will finish what he has started, and as we are reminded in verse 10, "Who has despised the day of small things?" No matter how slow the pace is or how small we have started, God will complete what he has started. Every obstacle shall be removed. Every mountain shall be made low.

Note that Zerubbabel spoke to the mountain. He already had the assurance of victory, and by faith, he commanded the mountain to become a plain. We can speak to our situation, and as we do so in faith, we will see every high place come down and every mountain leveled.

My Prayer

Father, I thank you that even when things seem to be moving slowly, you are still working. I will continue to hold on to your word because you are faithful to bring your words to pass, even when it seems to be taking longer. Help me to realize that your timing may be different from mine. I put my complete faith and trust in you and thank you for your faithfulness.

Day 15

PRAISE YOUR WAY TO VICTORY

But You are holy, enthroned in the praises
of Israel.
                              —Psalm 22:3 (NKJV)

It will seem strange to people to praise God for things we have not seen or received. Yet as children of God, we can take him at his word; and in faith, we praise him even for things we have not yet received.

We often need to praise him before we receive the victory. In 2 Chronicles 20, the Lord assured King Jehoshaphat of the victory over the Moabites and Ammonites. Once King Jehoshaphat received that word, he did not wait to see it before praising God. On the day of the battle, he arose early and advanced into the wilderness. He also appointed singers who would praise the Lord as they advanced. Verse 22 (NIV) says,

> As they began to sing and praise, the LORD set ambushes against the men of Ammon and Moab and Mount Seir who were invading Judah, and those men were defeated.

Acts 16 tells us of Paul and Silas being arrested, beaten, and thrown in jail for preaching the gospel. While in jail, their feet were bound and fastened in stocks. Nonetheless, Paul and Silas prayed and sang praises to God. As they praised, there came a huge earthquake, and the prison doors flung open, and everyone's chains became loose. Paul and Silas had the opportunity to escape. This came about because they praised God despite their circumstances.

In Psalm 22:3, the Bible tells us that God inhabits the praises of Israel. This means that when we praise God, he draws nearer to us. Let us not underestimate the power of our praise. Let us praise him even before we see the victory.

My Prayer

Dear Lord, I praise you today because of who you are. There is none like you. You are the Most High God and you are worthy to be praised. I praise you despite my circumstance. I praise you in the good times and in the bad times. I lift my voice to praise and worship you because you are indeed worthy to be praised.

Day 16

LAZARUS, COME FORTH!

Did I not tell you that if you believe you
will see the glory of God?
—John 11:40 (NIV)

Lazarus was the brother of Jesus's close friends Mary and Martha. The time came when Lazarus became ill. Jesus knew of his illness but did not go and heal him. The Bible lets us know that Jesus deliberately delayed it. Jesus wanted the disciples to see that he could not only heal the sick but could also raise the dead. Jesus did not go to Mary and Martha until four days later.

Although Lazarus was already dead, Martha said to Jesus, "But even now I know that whatever you ask from God, God will give to you." Yet that same Martha reacted with doubt when Jesus told the men to remove the stone.

We are often like Martha. We often say with our mouths that "God can do anything." It is almost like a buzzword. Yet in our hearts, we place a limit on that anything.

God can do anything if we believe. That is why Jesus reminded Martha that if she believed, she would see the glory of God. The glory of God refers to God's splendor, majesty, and infinite power, all of which are manifested through the performance of miracles and signs and wonders. We can truly experience this if we believe *in our hearts* and not just by saying it.

Jesus called Lazarus from the dead, and he came forth. In the same way, we can speak to any dead situation in our lives and see it come to life if we believe. Let us not just speak belief but let us also believe in our hearts. If we truly believe, this will be manifested in our actions and in our reactions. Only then will we see the glory of God.

My Prayer

Father, I thank you for your assurance that I will experience your glory if I believe. I say today that I truly believe that all things are possible through you. Nothing is impossible with you. I thank you that you have given me the same authority to speak to any dead situation and see it come to life. In faith, I command everything that has been lost in my life. To be restored, I command anything that has been broken to be fixed. I command every illness to leave my body in the name of Jesus.

Day 17

LITTLE BY LITTLE

> Little by Little I will drive them out before you.
>
> —Exodus 23:30 (NIV)

Does it seem sometimes that God is taking too long to do what he promised to do in your life? You've been exercising your faith and believing God to work on your behalf, but it looks like God is taking so long. He's not working fast enough.

We live in what is called a microwave culture, so we are used to things happening instantly or quickly. We know that God can and does work instantly. We have seen miraculous healings of people who instantly recovered. We have seen instant deliverances time and time again. However, God does not always work instantly; and when he chooses to work little by little, it is usually for our own good.

The Lord says this in Exodus 23:29. He told the children of Israel that he would drive out their enemies from the land he had promised them. Then he says,

> But I will not drive them out in a single year because the land would become desolate and the wild animals too numerous for you. Little by little I will drive them out before you until you have increased enough to take possession of the land. (NIV)

In Deuteronomy 7:22–23, the Lord again says,

> The Lord your God will drive out those
> nations before you little by little. You will
> not be allowed to eliminate them all at once
> or the wild animals will multiply around
> you. But the Lord your God will deliver
> them over to you throwing them into great
> confusion until they are destroyed. (NIV)

When we think that God is taking a bit long, know that he is still working, but he's working for our good. He sees ahead of us. He knows that the blessings he promised us cannot be given all at once because we are not prepared to receive them all at once.

In the book of Zechariah, God promised Zerubbabel that the temple would be rebuilt. In Zechariah 4:10, Zerubbabel received a vision of rebuilding the temple. Lots of people had lost hope for the rebuilding of the temple. However, in the vision, Zerubbabel was asked,

> For who has despised the day of small
> things? For these seven rejoice to see The
> plumb line in the hand of Zerubbabel.
> (NKJV)

In other words, it may have taken long for the temple to be rebuilt. There might have been discouragement. The foundation had been laid years before, but the temple was still incomplete. Nevertheless, we are reminded not to despise the days when nothing seems to be happening or when there is little movement toward where God has promised to take us. Do not despise those days because God is working little by little.

My Prayer

Dear Lord, it does seem sometimes that things are too long to happen in my life. Nonetheless, I continue to trust you and stand upon your word. I know that you will do what you promised to do because you are God and cannot lie. Give me the strength and the patience to wait. Open my eyes to see that you are working in my situation and helping me not to despise the days of small beginnings. I trust you to do what you said you would do, and I rejoice knowing that I will see your promises come to pass in my life.

IN THE MIDST OF THE STORM

> But when he saw that the wind was boisterous, he was afraid.
> —Matthew 14:30 (NKJV)

Whenever we are faced with a situation where God has promised us a breakthrough, it is easy to rejoice and give him praise as we see his hand at work. What if the tides change and things begin to go bad? It will then seem like God is no longer working. We may ask ourselves if we misunderstood the Lord when he said he would work things out. Do we then become fearful and doubt that God will come through for us? In the Bible, Peter's experience teaches us how disastrous those moments of doubt can be.

Peter had seen Jesus walking on the water, and he cried out to him, saying, "Lord, if it is you bid me come." Jesus told Peter to come, and immediately, Peter stepped out of the boat and began walking toward Jesus. Perhaps the sea was calm when Peter stepped out of the boat, so it was probably very easy for him to believe. This belief is what caused him to walk on water. Nonetheless, things began to get rough, and in Matthew 14:30, the Bible tells us,

But when he saw that the wind was boisterous, he was afraid and beginning to sink he cried out, "Lord save me." (NKJV)

Jesus stretched out his hand and caught him and then said,

O you of little faith, why did you doubt? (Matthew 14:31 NKJV)

Those are crucial words for us, why did you doubt? Peter did not doubt in the beginning, but when circumstances became rough, he began to doubt and then began to sink. The lesson is this: The Lord may give us peace about a situation. It may be about buying a property, taking a job, going someplace, or anything God puts before us. It doesn't mean that things will always go smoothly. When the tides begin to turn, it is important to keep our focus on Jesus and continue doing what he has called us to do.

Matthew 8:23–26 relates another situation of the disciples being in a boat. This time, Jesus was asleep; and a storm came, causing the disciples to become afraid. Again, Jesus rebuked them, saying,

Why are you fearful, O you of little faith? (NKJV)

Fear and doubt may hamper your success. If Jesus is with us, why should we fear or doubt that we will succeed? He is the God of the impossible. Tides may turn, and storms may come, but only fear and doubt will cause us to sink. Let us continue to trust him even in the midst of the storm.

My Prayer

Father, I come before you today in repentance for every time I have allowed doubt to creep into my mind. I reject the spirit of doubt today, and despite any difficult time I am experiencing, I continue to trust you. I know that storms do not last forever. You can keep me throughout every storm and throughout every difficulty. I draw strength from your word today, and I will continue to keep my eyes focused on you even in the midst of the storm because no storm is too rough for you.

Day 19

JESUS OUR MULTIPLIER

Surely blessing I will bless you and
multiplying I will multiply you.
—Hebrews 6:14 (NKJV)

One of the many miracles Jesus did while he walked on earth was to feed five thousand people using five loaves of bread and two fish. A crowd had stayed with Jesus all day, and they were hungry. The disciples told Jesus to send them away so that they could get food. The disciples obviously had not yet fully understood who they were dealing with. Wouldn't it be strange for the King of Kings, the provider of all things, to send people to another source for provision?

Jesus told the disciples to bring the five loaves and two fish. He then lifted them to heaven and blessed them. The food was then multiplied, and Jesus was able to feed five thousand people with only five fish and two loaves of bread and still had leftovers.

In the days of Elijah, there was a famine in Zarephath. Yet the Lord told Elijah to go to Zarephath, where there was a poor widow woman that would give him food. Elijah went to Zarephath as the Lord had directed him, and when he saw the woman, he asked her for water and bread. Her response was that she only had a handful of flour and a bit of olive oil. She was about to make a meal for herself and her son so that they would eat and then die.

Elijah told her to make bread for him first from what she had, and then she should make something for herself and her son for "this is what the Lord, the God of Israel says: 'The jar of flour will not be used up and the jug of oil will not run dry until the day the Lord send rain on the Land.'"

The woman did as Elijah said; indeed, the jar of flour was never used up, and the oil in the jar never dried up.

Our God is indeed a multiplier. Many other scriptures in the Bible talk about God multiplying the blessings of his people. For instance, Genesis 26:12 says,

> Then Isaac sowed in that land and received in the same year an hundredfold; and Lord blessed him. (KJV)

In Deuteronomy 30:16 (KJV), it says,

> In that I command thee this day to love the LORD thy God, to walk in his ways, and to keep his commandments and his statutes and his judgments, that thou mayest live and multiply.

Isn't it wonderful that he is the same yesterday as today? Our Lord can take what we have and multiply it. All it requires is for us to trust him with what we have.

My Prayer

Father, I thank you that you are a multiplier. Even when there is a lack, you are able not only to provide but also to multiply. I thank you that you are the same God of Elijah and that what you did yesterday you can do today. I thank you that you never change. And so I pray that I will know no lack. I pray that where I have little or barely enough that you will multiply. I pray that I will always have enough to fulfill my needs and the needs of others. I thank you that as I give unto others, you will multiply what I have so that I will continue to be a giver and blessing to others, all for the glory of your name.

WHOSE REPORT WILL YOU BELIEVE?

> And do not fear the people of the land, for
> they are bread for us. Their protection is
> removed from them, and the LORD is with
> us; do not fear them.
>
> —Numbers 14:9 (ESV)

God had told the children of Israel that he would take them to the Promised Land. This land had been promised to Abraham, and God intended to keep his covenant with Abraham's descendants.

As they approached the land, God told Moses to send twelve men to spy on the land. Numbers 13 tells us that the spies saw land with wonderful fruits such as grapes and pomegranates and figs. They realized that it was, indeed, a land flowing with milk and honey. After forty days, they returned and gave this report to Moses:

> We came to the land to which you sent us.
> It flows with milk and honey, and this is its
> fruit. However, the people who dwell in the
> land are strong, and the cities are fortified
> and very large. (Numbers 13:27 ESV)

Caleb, who was one of the spies, said,

> Let us go up at once and occupy it, for we are well able to overcome it. (Numbers 13:30 ESV)

Ten of the other men opposed him and said,

> We are not able to go up against the people, for they are stronger than we are. … The land, through which we have gone to spy it out, is a land that devours its inhabitants. (Numbers 13:32 ESV)

Of course, the entire camp of Israelites began to weep loudly, and they turned their wrath to Moses and Aaron. They chose to believe the report of the ten men and ignored the report of Caleb, who chose to stand on God's promise to give them the land. This caused the anger of God to burn against the Israelites. Not only were the ten spies killed, but also, God allowed the children of Israel to wander in the desert for forty years.

Are we like the children of Israel? Do we allow giants to cause us to doubt the promises of God? Your giant may be an incurable illness for which the doctor has given you a bad report. Your giant may also be in financial doom where there seems to be no way out of your economic difficulty. No matter how big the giants are, we must continue to stand on God's promises. Just like the children of Israel, doubt will cause us to miss out on the promises of God.

Let us choose to believe the promises of God. He has the final say, and no matter how large the giants loom over us, we will have what God says we will have once we believe.

My Prayer

Father, despite how impossible things may seem, I choose today to stand upon your word. I choose to believe you and not what the world is saying. I believe your report, not the doctor's report. I believe your report, not the report in the news. I am not afraid of anything that seems formidable because I know that you are the Lord of every situation and that through you, I am an overcomer. You have commanded us many times not to fear. I reject fear and keep my eyes on you because you have the final say.

Day 21

RAHAB, THE DO NOTHING

For the Egyptians shall help in vain and to no purpose. Therefore, I have called her Rahab-Hem-Shebeth.
—Isaiah 30:7 (NKJV)

In Isaiah 30, God condemns the children of Israel for looking to Egypt for help rather than looking to him. This is what the Bible says in Isaiah 30:1–5 (NIV):

> "Woe to the obstinate children," declares the Lord, "to those who carry out plans that are not mine, forming an alliance, but not by my Spirit, heaping sin upon sin, who go down to Egypt without consulting me, who look for help to Pharaoh's protection, to Egypt's shade for refuge. But Pharaoh's protection will be to your shame, Egypt's shade will bring you disgrace."

Egypt is likened today to worldly systems and idols. One way we put our trust in idols is when we depend on our money to get us through difficulties. Some people expect political leaders to provide solutions to problems. God wants his people to depend on him, not on the world. We are to seek God's direction and protection as the system of the world would fail us. In verse 7, Egypt is referred to as Rahab the do Nothing. In other words, a powerless Egypt that cannot protect itself. In the same way, the system of the world cannot protect us.

God is so angry when we put our trust in the world that he says that this sin will be met with destruction. What does God promise when we return to him and put our trust in him? He promises that we will weep no more. In verse 23, it says, "He will send rain for the seed we sow in the ground and the food that comes from the land will be rich and plentiful. Our cattle will feed in large pastures." In other words, when we trust only in the Lord, we will prosper and flourish and enjoy his protection.

My Prayer

Father, sometimes the world promises so much that it is sometimes tempting to follow the ways of the world and depend on worldly systems. I repent for any time I have placed my trust in anything or any person other than you. I look only to you for help, for only you have the answers to every situation that I am faced with. I seek refuge and protection from you and not from the world because worldly systems will fail, but you can never fail.

Day 22

ACTIVATING GOD'S BLESSINGS

> I will surely bless you, and I will surely multiply your offspring as the stars of heaven and as the sand that is on the seashore.
> —Genesis 22:1 (ESV)

God promised to bless Abraham and multiply his seed as the stars of heaven. What did Abraham do to obtain a promise of such a great blessing? It was his obedience. After blessing Abraham with a son after so many years of childlessness, God had now asked Abraham to sacrifice his only son. Abraham was obedient to God and was prepared to follow his command. Just as Abraham was about to sacrifice his son, God stopped him. Nonetheless, his willingness to obey God no matter what evoked a tremendous blessing that would last throughout the ages. In verse 18, God said,

> In your offspring shall all the nations of the earth be blessed, because you have obeyed my voice. (ESV)

Obedience is the key to activating the blessing of God. We see this in Deuteronomy 28, where Moses reminds the children of Israel that

> if you diligently obey the voice of the Lord your God, to observe carefully all His commandments which I command you today, that the Lord your God will set you high above all nations of the earth. And all these blessings shall come upon you and overtake you, because you obey the voice of the Lord your God. (NKJV)

Moses then outlines the many blessings that will be enjoyed. Among them, their bread basket will be blessed, the fruit of the ground and their body will be blessed, their enemies will be defeated before them, and everything they set their hand to will be blessed. The same blessings belong to us today once we walk in obedience to God's word.

The fact that Abraham was willing to obey God meant that he had great faith and trust in him. He knew that the god who was so faithful to provide him with a son after so many years would definitely reward him for his obedience. In the same manner, as we put our faith and trust in God, it becomes easy to obey his voice because we know that significant blessings will flow from our obedience.

My Prayer

Father, I come before you today with praise and thanksgiving. Thank you because you desire to bless me with many good things. I know that if I walk in obedience, you will withhold no good thing from me. I ask that you give me the strength to live my life in a manner that is pleasing to you so that I can truly enjoy the many blessings that are stored up for me. I thank you even now for those blessings in Jesus's name.

Day 23

HE WILL MAKE A WAY

> I am making a way in the wilderness and
> streams in the wasteland.
> —Isaiah 43:19 (NIV)

Our God is a waymaker. He says in Isaiah 43:19–20,

> I am making a way in the wilderness and
> streams in the wasteland. The wild animals
> honor me, the jackals and the owls, because
> I provide water in the wilderness and
> streams in the wasteland, to give drink to
> my people, my chosen, the people I formed
> for myself. (NIV)

In Isaiah 42:16, God says he will lead the blind in a way they do not know and turn the darkness before them into light and the rough places into level ground.

These scriptures give us hope that when things seem difficult and impossible, God is able to come through for us. He is the same God who parted the Red Sea and made a path for the children of Israel to pass through. He is the same God who shut the mouths of the lions when Daniel and his friends were thrown into the fiery furnace.

God has not changed, and he wants to deliver us out of hopeless situations. Do you believe he can do for you what he did before? It is up to you. If you have faith that God will do the impossible in your life, he will do it. The key is to take him at his word. It is he who is saying that he will make a way. He wants to make a way out of the sickness doctors have given up on. He wants to make a way out of financial struggles and debt. He wants to make a way out of broken relationships. He wants to make a way out of every wilderness situation that faces you. Therefore, take him at his word and believe him today.

My Prayer

Father, I come to you in the precious name of your Son, Jesus Crist. Thank you that you have said in your word that you will make a way for me. I believe your word, and I stand upon your word and promise today. I will not be moved by any difficult circumstance because I know that you will always come through for me. Thank you for your goodness toward me. In Jesus's name. Amen.

Day 24

KNOW YOUR WORTH

> But you are a chosen people, a royal priesthood.
>
> —1 Peter 2:9 (NIV)

Do you sometimes feel worthless or discouraged? From the moment we give our lives to Jesus, we become separated from the rest of the world, and we become an heir to the everlasting kingdom of the King of Kings. Here is what the Bible says about us in 1 Peter 2:9 (NIV):

> But you are a chosen people, a royal priesthood, a holy nation, God's special possession, that you may declare the praises of Him who called you out of darkness into His wonderful light.

That should make you feel like royalty!

Ephesians 1:13 tells us that God has put his seal on us, and that seal is the Holy Spirit. That seal marks and sets us apart as his. Furthermore, that seal is a down payment that acts as a guarantee of our future inheritance!

Paul reminds us in 1 Corinthians 6:20 that we were bought with a price. It was a high price that involved the shedding of innocent blood. 1 Peter 1:18 tells us that "we were not redeemed with corruptible things like silver and gold … but by the precious blood of Christ as a lamb without blemish and without spot."

These scriptures and many more tell us that we are precious in the sight of God. Our salvation came at a high price, which is the shedding of the precious blood of Jesus. God has set us apart for his glory and honor. We must never let the world make us feel like we are worthless. We are royalty, we are seated with him in heavenly places, we are the salt of the earth, and we are fearfully and wonderfully made!

My Prayer

Father, I thank you for the finished work on the cross. I thank you that you have chosen me and that you have given me your Holy Spirit and that I am seated in heavenly places with Christ Jesus. This is all because of your love for me, and I give you praise and thanks for such love. Help me to always remember who I am and who I belong to and to live in a manner that is in keeping with my inheritance in you. In Jesus's name. Amen.

ULTIMATE UNCONDITIONAL LOVE

> He who did not spare his own Son, but gave him up for us all—how will he not also, along with him, graciously give us all things?
>
> —Romans 8:32 (NIV)

How many of us will sacrifice our son or daughter to save a friend? I am sure the answer is none. None of us would do that because as much as we love our friends, we love our children more. Yet God sacrificed his Son for us. This is the ultimate testimony of his love for us. If God loved us so much to send his Son as a sacrifice, what else would he not do for us? As Paul says in Romans 8:31–33 (NIV),

> If God is for us, who can be against us? He who did not spare his own son but delivered Him up for us all how shall he not with Him also freely give us all things?

This is a reminder that we need not worry and fret about what the world throws at us. When the world accuses us, God will bring justification; when the world condemns us, Christ will intercede for us. We are assured of God's ultimate and unconditional love. His love for us is so deep that he sent his Son as a sacrificial lamb. We have no need to fear anything that the world brings to us because that same Son who was sacrificed for us is now interceding for us. We are assured of victory. Only continue to believe and rest in him.

My Prayer

Father, thank you for your unconditional love for me that you sent your Son to die for me. Because of your love for me, I know I do not need to fear anything. I reject all fear and doubt and I place my complete trust in you, for I know that you will never fail me.

OUR WARRIOR KING

The Lord will fight for you, and you have
only to be silent.
—Exodus 14:14 (ESV)

The Bible describes the Lord as a man of war. This description
was given by Moses and the children of Israel when the Lord
parted the Red Sea for them to cross over and the Pharaoh's
army drowned. Moses had earlier told the children of Israel
that the Lord would fight for them and that they only needed
to be silent. They had been consumed with fear when they
saw the Egyptian army approaching them, but God indeed
fought for them and gave them victory.

Isn't it wonderful to know that the King of Kings
fights for us? It is inevitable that we will face obstacles and
hardships, but it is comforting to know that we have a God
on our side who engages in battles on our behalf.

In Deuteronomy 20, Moses told the children of Israel
that whenever they went out to battle, they should not be
afraid of the enemy's horses and chariots and of an army
larger than their own, for the same Lord who brought them
out of Egypt is with them. He further told them that just
before the battle, the priest would remind them that "the
Lord your God is He who goes with you to fight for you
against your enemies and give you the victory."

God is still a man of war. He is our Warrior King. Let

us not be afraid of what the enemy throws at us. Our Lord will fight for us, and we are assured of the victory.

My Prayer

Father, I come before you in the name of Jesus. I thank you because you fight my battles. You said in your word that you will fight for me. I thank you today that you go before me and that you will never leave or forsake me. Because of that, I am victorious over every plot of the enemy. I thank you for this. In Jesus's name. Amen.

Day 27

WE WILL GET WHAT WE SEE

> All the land that you see I will give to you
> and your offspring forever.
> —Genesis 13:15 (ESV)

Abraham and Lot journeyed together to Bethel. Both men had become wealthy with livestock and could no longer dwell together. After they separated, the Lord told Abraham he wanted to bless him exceedingly. It is well known that God told Abraham, "All the land that you see I will give to you and your offspring forever." Apart from the natural meaning of those words, there is also a spiritual significance to this scripture. I believe the blessings we receive from God are tied to the vision that we have. God cannot bless us beyond what we envisage because we would be unable to cope with the blessings. God told Abraham to "lift up your eyes and look from where you are." That means that before Abraham could receive the blessings, he had to see them and see beyond his present circumstances.

In the same manner, before we can receive anything from God, we have to see it and envisage it spiritually. We have to know what that blessing looks like. How else can we believe God for it? And yes, God can give even more than we can see because the Bible tells us that he can do above and beyond what we can ask or think.

Only when we can envisage it, we can believe God for it and then receive that which we have believed God for. We cannot believe God for something unless we know that it exists.

The formula is this: First, we look, then we see, then we believe, and then we receive. Our prayer should be to ask God to expand our vision. As our vision expands, we can see what God can potentially do for us, and through us, we can then believe and trust him to bring these things to pass.

My Prayer

Father, I thank you that your desire is to bless me abundantly. I pray that you help me widen my vision and expand my thinking so that I can believe you for big things. Forgive me for placing limits on my life and for placing limits on what you are able to do through me. Thank you for your enlarged vision and abundant blessings. In Jesus's name, amen.

Day 28

ARE YOU DRESSED FOR BATTLE?

> Therefore, put on the full armor of God, so
> that when the day of evil comes, you may
> be able to stand your ground, and after you
> have done everything, to stand.
> —Ephesians 6:13 (NIV)

As children of God, we are expected to stand strong against the enemy. This means that we need to prepare to fight battles.

We know that the weapons of our warfare are not carnal. Our war is spiritual; therefore, our weapons must be spiritual. We are in a constant battle. The Bible says that our afflictions are many, but the Lord will deliver us from them all. However, we are required to stand. In other words, we should not back down from the enemy. We must, however, focus on the words that come before *stand*. The entire phrase says, "Having done all, stand."

How, then, are we to stand? We are to ensure that we are fully dressed for battle. Ephesians 6:14 tells us what our battle gear consists of. We must ensure that our battle gear consists of truth, righteousness, readiness, peace, faith, and salvation; and we must be grounded in his word so that we can speak to our situation. Only then can we stand firm against the enemy.

It makes no sense to stand against the enemy without our battle gear. We will be defeated. A soldier does not go to war without weapons and then stands against the enemy with no protective gear. That would be suicidal. Likewise, we as Christians should always be dressed for battle; and once we are dressed, we can stand firm against the enemy and be assured victory. Let us don our battle gear!

My Prayer

Father, thank you that you have told us in your word how to defeat the enemy. We are in a constant battle against the enemy, but you have told us how to protect ourselves. Today I accept and obey your word and put on your full armor. I will always carry your truth, righteousness, readiness, peace, faith, and salvation. I thank you that the enemy has no power against me as I am fully dressed in your armor.

THE GOD OF THE BREAKTHROUGH

The Lord has broken through my enemies
before me like a breakthrough of water.
—2 Samuel 5:20 (NKJV)

The Philistines were a constant thorn in the flesh of the Israelites. Throughout the Old Testament, we read of their constant wars with Israel. They were like bullies in a schoolyard. The Philistines were relentless, constantly going on the offensive against Israel. We see one encounter between the Philistines and Israel in 1 Samuel 17. Saul and his men were terrified by the threats of the giant Goliath, who fought on the side of the Philistines. Nonetheless, despite Goliath's size, David, who was at that time a mere shepherd boy could defeat him and cut his head off.

In 2 Samuel 5:20, David again encountered the Philistines, who came out to battle with him after they heard that he had been anointed king. David inquired of the Lord whether he should go up against them. The Lord assured David of the victory. When David defeated the Philistines, he gave God the glory and said,

The Lord has broken through my enemies
before me like a breakthrough of water. (2
Samuel 5:20 NKJV)

He then named the place of battle Baal-perazim, meaning the "Lord breaks through."

The concept of bursting or breaking through gives the idea of a sudden force powerful enough to destroy something strong and formidable, like an iron or a stone wall. Given the strength of the Philistine army, defeating them was, indeed, a breakthrough.

The defeat of the Philistines required strong and powerful forces to break through their stronghold. The Lord was that force. He was the God of the breakthrough then and is still the God of the breakthrough. We may have thorns in our flesh today. These may come in many forms. No matter how formidable the circumstance or how strong the giants are in our lives, the God of the breakthrough can tear down the walls so that we can walk through victoriously.

My Prayer

Father, thank you that you are the same God who helped David win the battle against the Philistines. You are still the God of the breakthrough. I bring every difficult and formidable situation before you. I declare that in the same way, you gave David the breakthrough, you are about to give me the breakthrough. No situation is too difficult for you. I thank you for the manifestation of the breakthrough in my life. Even now, I rejoice at the work of your hands, and I declare and receive victory over every situation. In Jesus's name. Amen.

REMOVE THE ACCURSED THING

Neither will I be with you anymore, unless
you destroy the accursed from among you.
—Josh. 7:12 (NKJV)

Do you believe in God for blessings? Do you believe that your blessings have been delayed? Maybe it's time to check the camp of your life to see what is holding up your blessing.

When God brought the children of Israel out of Egypt, he promised them a land that he would bless them with. Yet it took forty years before they could enter that land. In Deuteronomy 2:13, we are told that the time it took to cross the Valley of Zered was thirty-eight years until the generations of the men of war had all been consumed from the midst of the camp just as the Lord had sworn to them to destroy them from the midst of the camp.

In Joshua 7, after the children of Israel finally entered Jericho, one would expect that God would continue to bless and help them defeat their enemies. Under the leadership of Joshua, the men went up against Ai and were defeated. This came as a surprise to Joshua as God had promised to give them victory in overcoming their enemies.

It turned out that there was sin in their midst. Contrary to what God had commanded the Israelites, Achan kept the accursed things from the land of Jericho. The accursed things were objects used in idol worshipping. God wanted his people to have no part in idol worshipping, so they were not to keep the idols.

After their defeat, these are the words God spoke to Joshua, "There is an accursed thing in your midst, O Israel you cannot stand before your enemies until you take away the accursed thing from among you."

It is the same with our lives. The examples of Israelites wandering for forty years and the defeat at Ai show us that we can hinder and delay our blessings. Is there an accursed thing in your life? Is there doubt, negativity, complaining, anger, bitterness, fornication? Anything that God forbids will hinder us from receiving the blessing. We need to get rid of the accursed thing so that we can step into our blessings.

My Prayer

Father, I come before you today, and I confess that I harbor attitudes and things that may be hindering my blessings. Today I relinquish every bad attitude and sinful lifestyle. If there are any objects in my home that should not be there, I ask that you reveal them to me so that I can get rid of everything that brings displeasure to you. I want to enjoy the fullness of your blessings, and so I ask for your help in removing every hindrance from my life. In Jesus's name, I pray. Amen.

Day 31

STANDING ALONE
WITH JESUS

> I have been very zealous for the Lord God Almighty. The Israelites have rejected your covenant, torn down your altars, and put your prophets to death with the sword. I am the only one left, and now they are trying to kill me too.
>
> —1 Kings 19:10 (NIV)

Are you prepared to stand alone with Jesus? You might be the only one among your friends who refuse to engage in sin and insist on living according to God's word. This can often be a lonely road. In 1 Kings 19:10, Elijah cried out to the Lord and said,

> I have been very jealous for the LORD God of hosts: for the children of Israel have forsaken thy covenant, thrown down thine altars, and slain thy prophets with the sword; and I, even I only, am left; and they seek my life, to take it away.

Elijah was obviously frustrated that everyone seemed to prosper in their wickedness, and he seemed to be the only one who stood firm. Yet this caused his life to be in danger.

In many instances, being alone in standing for God causes people to turn away or compromise. In John 6, when Jesus taught in the synagogue, some of his disciples said, "This is a hard teaching. Who can accept it?" Many of them turned back and no longer followed him.

Noah must have felt very alone being a righteous man in a community of wicked men. When God commanded him to build an ark, one can imagine the number of scoffers and naysayers. In Genesis 7:1 (NIV), God told Noah,

> Go into the ark, you and your whole family, because I have found you righteous in this generation.

This suggests that Noah stood out among others in his generation and community. Yet he persisted in building the ark as God commanded him. Eventually, God proved himself faithful.

Yet we are never really alone. Jesus told us that he would never leave or forsake us. In 1 Kings, God showed Elijah that he was not really alone. First, God showed him that he was with him and appeared in a small voice. Then God showed Elijah that there were others who had not bowed down to Baal.

Never be afraid to stand alone for Jesus because, in actual fact, you are never alone. Jesus is always with you, and he always provides help.

My Prayer

Father, I confess that sometimes I do feel alone. Sin is so much accepted in the world today that standing up for righteousness often seems odd. Despite this, I will continue to stand up for righteousness even if I am the only one among my family or friends. I know that you are always with me, and I know that if I put you first, you will bless me and keep me in ways that everyone will know that your hand is upon my life. I thank you that you are always with me. In Jesus's name, amen.

Printed in the United States
by Baker & Taylor Publisher Services